The River People

THE RIVER PEOPLE

poems

Polly Buckingham

LOST HORSE PRESS
Sandpoint, Idaho

Copyright © 2020 by Polly Buckingham.

Cover Painting: Andrea Dezsö. Paintings by Ms. Dezsö are found online at
    www.andreadezso.com.
Author Photo: Heath Herrick.
Book Design: Christine Lysnewycz Holbert.

FIRST EDITION

This and other fine LOST HORSE PRESS titles may be viewed on our website at
www.losthorsepress.org.

LIBRARY OF CONGRESS CATALOGING-IN-PUBLICATION DATA

Cataloging-in-Publication Data may be obtained from the Library of Congress.
ISBN 978-1-7333400-7-6

For Molly, in memory

Table of Contents

Florida Moon

Constant Rain

White Train

The Last Day of January

FLORIDA MOON

Savior

I hold the door open
and all the people come in. They come
carrying their heads in their hands,
looking for beds, for plaster skies.

The doorknob feels cold in my palm
and I hold the door open.
They crawl in dragging their luggage,
arms, legs, and sheets to cover their faces.

A thin man brings a rope with burnt ends.
Cigarettes fall from his shirttails.
I hold the door open
and his shoe falls at the threshold.

Fat ones come with holes in their chests
and even if I could close the door,
my one hand will always touch the round
completeness of my face, and with the other

I will hold open the door.

The Day Picking Oranges Became Illegal

Balancing on a branch,
I filled my shirt with oranges.
But the tree began to shake,
and sirens filled the thin air
like manatees calling.
Orange traffic lights fell from my hands.
I hid my face in the leaves and

dreamed about stucco houses
overrun by cats and wisteria.
Bleached scallop shells
and bone white sand dollars blazed
in the shafts of light
which broke through the tiles
like rifts along the ocean floor.

When I was a child, Florida was the land
that rejected houses
and spit them into the smoky air.
Brush fires raced through March nights
leaving ash scattered across our yard.

Now the meaning of vast
has become orange trees in rows.
Strangers rape women who used to ride
horses bareback in the sand.
I am alone, watching
odd lights along tacky beach shores
like a child who has seen
a ghost with a white disc face
through a crack in the closet door.

Here in the White Room

full of silence and space,
wide like ice and snow, flocks
of birds, and street mobs,
I have a small wish to be

large. I hold up my hands
where I have seen his face,
but my palms slap ceiling,
and my head hits wall.

This is the window
where I saw his eyes—cave
mouths in the silver night,
round as manholes

in a rainy street. Outside
midgets weave in and out
of traffic, and stoplights
blink like the giant's red eyes

slowly opening and closing.

Middle Beach

You are a note without a body
in the underwater hum,
a mirage on palm fronds,

a pink conch inside,
a soft oyster offered
on round bread.

On the beach road Venetian blinds
crack open. Gulls hover gray
against the white hotel.
Someone throws bread crumbs.

Light pours through the keyhole
crack in my wall. I press
one eye over the hole.
Many white birds scatter like
doves in a sand dollar,

and I receive you, my body
a murex, whelk, moonshell.

Florida Morning

We wake to the smell of gardenia.
We float white flowers in a blue bowl.

At night when we follow the shore
handfuls of cold fade into stars.

Steam rises from the groves
coating each orange in a woolen haze.

We press each other between the sheets
and rise like ocean swells, then fade

as a ghost might float into morning.

Floating Face Up

On Simonton Street
teal breasted birds laugh
above the Bodega
as I buy Mogen Davids
from Aunt Lolly's Grocery.

Painted wooden parrots perch
in Poinciana trees
sipping on whiskey stems.
I pass them
and walk into

night,
slip naked and cold
into water.
Birds fall all about me.

The Fish Devour Us, Key West

Minnows bite cigarette butts,
heads breaking the surface,
all yellow eyes and large lost pupils.
As the tide drops, we see
coral, grass, sea cucumber.

A missile painted on a road
covered in tidewater
points toward the Atlantic Horizon.
We touch the center of a sea anemone.
Its mouth closes around us.

A spider sleeps in the center of a web
strung across mangrove branches.
We read nightmares in the hieroglyphics
on its white back and count
eight red star spikes,
a child's drawing of a dark sun.

Our paddle strikes a sea robin
hidden in mangrove roots.
Purple fluid stains the coral
white reflection of the surface.
Here at night are barracuda,
and the navy beaches become
graveyards for horseshoe crabs.

The tiny green fish grow larger,
their electric skeletons white.
As our raft descends with the tide,
we listen to the traffic
on Roosevelt Boulevard.

Hungry Guppies

He likes dinosaurs more than fish
'cause dinosaurs don't exist.
The walls around his bed crowd in
like guppies crowd the tank.

He wishes there weren't so many fish.
Won't they ever stop
pushing against the glass
like too many birds in the sky?

His third grade teacher, Mrs. Hanafan,
says there are too many cats on Crete,
and he's seen the pictures of them
sitting tense on windowsills,
so it must be true.

Now the guppies cover his walls
like ink blots. They cover the white sheets,
slip under his head onto the pillow.
They cover his face and fill his mouth.
And they cover the light.

Guppies and guppies and guppies
real as the children
standing in line at Old Orchard
shopping mall waiting for Santa —

so many children.

Morning Wash

Everything is blue and white—

your eyes, the water glass,
white dolphin on a blue horizon,
Alaskan ice and snow, blue

bottles behind a dark window,
drawn shades facing waves like
eggstones in the undercurrent,
sun on the esplanade, white fish

flesh tossed in the bay, egrets
picking pinfish from a bait pail,
curved half moon bellies,

your coral necklace and a blue
print band around your Panama hat
with a single white feather,

and sheets in the morning water light.

Potting Roses

Roses: lavender Angel Face
and pink Peace,
this glow called color
appears on a clear
morning, and I wonder
about wings.

"Angel," you said, and you
squeezed the emptiness out of me.
"You'll have to let it go."

I suppose this is the peace
after a summer rain
when mist rises above the roses
and the white faces
of angels dissipate.

Hotel Florida

Have dinner with me
at the Vinoy. You can't
climb the fence barefoot. I'll bring you
shoes from the church.

I have bologna and bread from Mr. C's
Discount Grocery, an avocado
from the sidewalk,
cigarettes, a cockleshell ashtray.
You bring the booze.

We can choose a room over the bay,
maybe 216? Sometimes chameleons
climb in from the palm frond
that breaks through the screen
and skitter across the broken mattress.

Tonight, the moon will fill
216, and by midnight
it will have risen past the one
large window—we could move to 316

or 416. We can talk as dark
fills the cracks and palmetto bugs
rush across the floor, talk about
how the streets are death with an

empty white face, how I found you
standing on the corner,
one blackened foot hovering
over the road. How you couldn't
move.

Beaten Blues

Don't call.
I don't want to cry.
The fan's moaning
because the screws are loose,
and the floor's wet with rain.

Why'd you leave me?
The fan's loose, and I'm
on the floor watching
my big hands,
rain on my face.

Don't call, by morning
the fan will dry the floor,
and I can stop the rain
with my hands.

Hello Lucy

Outside the moon
is wider than a dime
and we can move in patterns
of the constellations.

I know how your body
becomes hollow, how this place
is filled with
you and nothing,
Lucy and the room.

I can fill you
with round white stars.
Fold back the sheet,
pull me in.

Hold me as if I were
morning wrapped in a blanket.

The Upstairs Window

Mornings, still drunk, I crouch
on the cracked bathroom tile. I see
a thin woman with a moon face
opening and closing her raccoon eyes.

A passionate, affected woman
in a Queen of Spades costume
hides from a strong man's mallet
in a carnival's fun house of mirrors.

An old woman from the Hebrides
kneels where a red light
seeps through a crack. Palms
face to face, in black, she chants.

When sparrows cover the sky, I see
the crosses I've carved in the plaster walls.
I close the bathtub curtain,
and I close the bathroom door.

Wind echoes in the high corners.

Easter Morning

We fell asleep with the TV on,
and the Pope spoke
in our morning dreams.

Lamb of God who takes away
the sins of the world,

Slats of shutter light
fell across your body,
and through the window
I saw an old house
crowded with birds.

have mercy on us.

We crossed our bodies
under the sheets
and filled each other
with a white moment where
movement seemed unreal.

Lamb of God who takes away
the sins of the world,

The bells at St. Peter's rang.

grant us peace.

We bent our knees, mine inside yours,
and listened.

Waking in a Church in Cedar Key
first day of ground war, 1990

I'm standing outside
of an old white house. I look through
circles of dust on the windows,
and my feet recover themselves

with soot. I walk in full
sunlight knowing the silence
of awkward, wooden

wings lifting and falling.

Christmas Morning

A white bird fell
from the telephone wire.
I dropped the second rock—
first shot's the best.

At Christmas we sang
about turtle doves,
and on the way home
I saw the turtles by the side
of the road, too slow
to cross.

Father died five years ago.
I was three, don't remember
a thing. Someone told me today
about the stretcher, the sheet,
and the Christmas tree,
about the lump in his head
growing slow

After You're Gone

I'm standing in refrigerator light
pouring water into a blue glass
when a white van pulls up.
I peer under the blind,
and a large man steps into the drive
carrying flowers.
I look away and wait.
No one comes.
And then the drive's empty.
Everything still smells of flowers.

I don't look out my windows anymore.
I don't think about you
and music and the beach,
about red skies,
dolphin falling,
the rough horizon line
I saw through your binoculars
and a new cold evening.

And I don't remember the year
my father gave me an aquarium.
He made me close my eyes
and pressed my palms
against the glass. "Guess."
All the fish died.
All I remember now
is how to close my eyes.

Baby's Gone Away

Christmas Day Baby and I and the black dog walked down to Straub Park. Baby had put a tiny bit of hope on her pretty little face. I was drinking a beer in one hand and carrying the rest of the six pack in the other, my arm around Baby. Each time I took a sip of beer, my elbow'd pull Baby's face closer to mine, and she'd kiss me. The black dog wandered around the benches, his big head bent to the grass.

Baby said, "Let's watch *The Sound of Music* tonight."

"Sure, Baby," I said.

"Let's go sit by the camels," she said.

The nativity scene was human-sized with real almost camel-sized camels. Mary and Joseph and the wise men and the shepherds, their plastic faces lit with white sunlight, gazed into the palm frond manger. A sheep, its legs curled under itself, looked past the manger and out at Tampa Bay. Three palm trees hung still against a blue sky. Baby was wearing a tank top and men's swimming trunks with red hibiscus blossoms on them, and I was in my corduroy bus boy surfer shorts and the black t-shirt I'd ripped the sleeves off of.

As we got closer, Baby said, "Someone's stolen the Jesus."

A coconut fell and rolled across the grass, bounced onto the seawall and plunk over the edge like a bag of kittens. The black dog watched.

"Oh no," Baby said, all that Christmas hope gone from her face. I put my beers down, held Baby tight, and kissed her soft straw-colored head.

Bubba and the Pinfish

Bubba the night janitor lets me in.
He promises there'll be a crowd,
but the crowd still hasn't come.
In the elevator he pushes third floor
then presses his palm against the window.
The inside of the shaft falls away
on the other side of the glass.

He tells me about the artists who usually
perform. A girl with a cartoon face
sings about killing the queen in the mirror.
Bubba thinks she's a stray angel
who hit the stage wires and fell.
A short man with a beard tells stories
about disappearing trolls and bridges
that vanish in daylight, and one lonely poet
writes of whores and handles on ceiling fans.
Sometimes Bubba reads a poem.
The crowd's friendly. Anyone
can join. The audience lies on pillows in the dark,
and the artists stand in a dim spotlight.

But the crowd hasn't come tonight,
and the upstairs theater is under construction.
One wall is half painted blue, brush strokes
bold as finger paint. The other is red brick,
and everything is evenly lighted.

Bubba sits on the bottom step
and pulls a poem from his pocket.
"The Klutz." He watches his feet, his eyes
sunken and round like a drowning boy's.

"The Klutz is tall and thin.
Everyone hates him.
Everyone should run."

A young man's deep chorus
to an empty room.
The other side of laughter is pain.

"The Klutz caught a pinfish
that pulled him clean out of his boat
and dragged him across the bay
where he struck
a piling, tore down a dock,
and smacked against the seawall."

My claps echo in the lighted room
as Bubba folds up the battered blue-inked pages.
He takes my seat, and now I'm alone
on this step. I read a poem about love
and one about rain.

"Love is the soft banging
of white shadows on the ceiling,
a distance I call my own,
my face and the moon alone."

When I look up from my colorless page,
crabs run sideways across the floor,
and Bubba's feet are wet and coated with sand.
Behind him fish with silver and green gills
swim on a flat surface. I want to ask,

Bubba, do you have days when colors seem strange?

"Outside the window
faces pass like sheets
in a storm. Rain touches
one side of the glass."

Can you hear the world underwater?
What does silence
at the end of a pinfish line
feel like?

There was supposed to be a crowd,
but now there's only Bubba and me
on this one small step—

When you're underwater, do you know
when it's raining?

RainSong

On Highway 24 near the Suwannee and Cedar Key,
they say chickens cross the road to show armadillos
that it can be done. She was watching the rain
when the armadillo hit her muffler, young girl driving
into a trap, remembering hands that held her one drunk night
and a cool voice that drifts across the Cedar Key boardwalk.
She sees his face in rain, the face she's formed over
and over since the night on a tin roof they made
movement stop and everything had been clear.

Now the sound of his guitar races through the streets
throbbing like a train against the rail, like a fiddle lost
in its frenzy. She stands outside The Cedar's
listening. His whiskey glass on the window ledge separates
inside from out. His face falls away from his voice, his body
disconnected from his song, her soul removed from the comfortable
harmony of connected parts. She's holding back a scream
for the armadillo, and it hasn't stopped raining.

There's no place to hide, only the rain
slapping her face, the bridge over oyster beds,
and a man's voice filling her with the silence
of white cattle ibis against a gray sky. The island

whines with the night's rainsong. When evenings
wind down in Cedar Key, it's shots at the L & M.
She's been walking in the rain, and he's slack faced.
A raging woman drinking vodka and ice
slips him her hand. Minutes whir like tequila spinning
into glasses. The cue ball splits the others, and bar voices
ring like breaking glass. He's mumbling curses, and it
hasn't stopped raining. When the last lights flash at the L & M,
he follows the raging woman into the street.

In Cedar Key when you have no place, you sleep
in your car on the beach. And when the sun rises, you try
to eat at Cook's Café. She's slack faced, starving, staring up
at motel windows, mumbling curses. She spills
her coffee. The cup breaks on the floor like
the armadillo shell split open in the road. In Cedar Key,
love is trapped in a bottle, and young girls break open
as easily as rain falls in the street.

CONSTANT RAIN

The Big State

The clouds are gathering
stones and building storms.
There is a grayness here and
my arms ache from standing so long
like a moth with raised wings.
I don't remember where the screen door is
or when I walked out.

All I know is that light is most important,
and I will stay here and wait,
holding my wings open.

We Need the Rain

in memory of Duane Davis

I once swam in a mountain
lake half-covered in ice,
a hole between black peaks
and snow like the gray
side of a dream.
I squatted on an island
rock pressing my face
against air, staring
through a window from
the other side of warmth.

Tonight, steam rises
from these hot springs
and you wipe the rain
from my face with your finger.
We talk about bright moss,
alive, wet and clean.
Northern lights warm
the sky. We look for lights
in the water and find
each other. There is no window
between your face and mine.

315 West Marine, Astoria

From this porch
the street stretches to the river,
the mountains spread their arms
to receive the clouds, and mist
plays beneath the floorboards.
From here the world is as close
as it is from any other porch
in any city, under any sky.

From this porch I count pigeons
on the roof of the brown warehouse,
and the bridge over the river
owns the air. The angle of roofs
is different here, pigeons squat closer
to the gutters, and colors
are foreign and unique. Tulips open
like hungry young women, and
gray liquid life sweeps the porch.
The wood, soaked through,
becomes moss and dirt. The hillside
with its terraces of flowers stumbles
eager and weeping with growth.

Emptying Each Day

The light in my closet
fills slowly with brown water.
Each day it rises,
and each day
I mark my losses as a parent
measures a child's height
on the wall.
Upstairs a small girl stomps her feet.
Her mother is at the sink.
I know this because
water drips from the ceiling
around the rim of the light fixture.
I remember a fish I had,
how the water in the bowl turned brown
and the fish died.
I stare at the fishbowl
in my closet filling
with the sludge from old pipes.
The girl upstairs shrieks.
There is never enough attention.
Her mother is too tired to play,
her father is gone,
and too many people
come and go through her long days.
I am far from home.
Sometimes I see the child
peeking in my windows.
I'm empty inside.

Landscape

This year my sister cut
herself again and again, and this year
you moved away. This year
when I was tired from feeling
and trying to understand,
I'd bow my head against your shoulder
and the world would seep
slowly out.

Together we drove across the desert.
I told you my sister could not weep.
The white of the Salt Flats,
expanding like a piece of paper
without edges, was the very same
white inside my heart. I told you
how some days she was a person I knew,
and others no one I recognized.
Escalante canyon
dropped off the edge of the road
into what could be forever
but isn't.

The Coral Pink Sand Dunes
were unreal, though
this year everything
expands the world of real,
red rocks the shape of giant skulls
with room enough inside
for one curled person.
That could be me. Yesterday, we drove
along the Vermillion Cliffs—
the Colorado River far below.

I left you in the desert.
Every moment the distance between us
grows, but you still feel close.
Central Nevada is inside me as if
someone had folded a sheet of paper
and changed everything.
There is a bit of obsidian
beside the road. Could a tear
have turned to rock?

Outside my window

a low moon
counts my losses.
My heart
cannot hold
another spoonful
of gone.

Disappearing
into the too
clear evening,
blackbirds
rise and separate,
and the branches
that reach for them
fall.

Outside the window
my body
is the moon.
My sad spirit,
its chin
in its palms,
watches.

Not the smallest
part of me
could swallow
even the
smallest
loss.

Grieving at the Longest Traffic Light in the World

The light will never change.
I examine my hand on the steering wheel
in the terrible heat of stop, a half moon
in the curve of my finger,
holes remaining from stitches.

I think of how long it takes for hands to heal,
how grief is a disc of silence
I am passing through,
pausing to prevent infection,
how the wound from your absence
will come out from the whiteness of shock
and the delicate skin
will tape itself to the life.

The Ferry Ride

Sometimes I take a ferry
rowed by a boatman with a gray beard
and cartoon face. On the other side
I run through wet trees
and sleep on beaches.
I collect berries and mushrooms
and mussels near a small town
filled with all the people I once knew
where the person I was once lived:
cobbled streets and mossy forest floors,
empty Victorians with broken windows,
sea creatures on the shore
waiting for the tide.

Now there is only this forever ferry ride,
the breeze moving my hair so steadily
it feels still, the constant
face of the ferryman gazing past me,
the water expanding gray and blue
and the sun repeating itself
across the surface.

I live in a city on a hill.
I am a still person whose
life has been a series of windows.
The back and forth of the ferry
negates itself, and the glassy water
opens with each stroke of the oars.

MoonBoy

A year tomorrow he's been gone.
An earthquake shook the windows.
Outside the full moon jumped in the sky.
Once I dreamed him a child
lifted into the air by a crowd of people.
Once we sat on a log and the moon rose orange
over our little town of colored houses,
over water, sand, and jetty.
If I could hold this inside me, he said.
I drew the evening in crayon.
Ice clicks in his glass, tinny
through the phone. I feel far away.
He says it's not so far,
but I know I will not
see him again, and now
there is no longer room to say so.
I look through the window of a closed store
at dozens of empty beds.
It's spring and the moon is high.

Night Life

The night before last
the village was all shot up
you and I on our stomachs
sparks spraying dirt around
the edges of our faces across
the road a truck explodes
you press your hands over
my ears when we run there is
nothing but bramble how could
we leave home with no trail?

Last night a woman hands me
a cat the cat scratches
x's over my eyes a giant dog
leaps like the cow's shadow
I fly too close to the moon
wax burns my arms the earth
a magnet pulls me face first
toward its dusty night roads.

Tonight. There is a river.
A wide brown river with waxy
green leaves along the bank.
The water a slowly moving
hammock holds my sore back.
Rapids bubble up warm
from the muddy bottom
and small fish exhale
glossy little worlds
that turn in the current.

Tomorrow night I'll find you.
I'll say I know a place and
you'll say I need a place and
we'll step into a child's map.
From above, blue rivers curl
around little islands, green
trees and yellow beaches.
We'll float through mangroves.
We are old white shells
silent and full of holes.

the old city

to save the old city
I bought a room with a red door
at the bottom of an alley stairway

a room where flies buzz out of cracks
and poisonous house spiders hide
in piles of junk

the *City Newspaper* warns against
digging up graveyards

a woman on the alley steps
brushes dirt off her lips
give you a penny if you take my dog

white mold grows across gritty brick
God is watching the woman says
the dog licks my hand

the polls say 90% of City residents
would bury the whole mess

still I believe light shines
through dark places

belief is a warm room after a rain shower
and a white robe
waiting on a rusted hook

Between Winter and Spring

Nocturne

red butterflies
above a white trail

a deer bounds through fern
swords triangle the sun

a man cuts his hair
a woman runs a tub-
ful of water

i swim across the yard
flies dance on surface ice

the night is a deep-sea skate
skimming over sand

Constant Rain

the end of a circle reaches
around for its curve

snow like blown
dandelions spins out-

side a wood framed window
trees angle
and crooked kindling

intersects
the day's lattice

WHITE TRAIN

The Capacity of a Dog to Be Still

There is a secret between
us silent as the veins on a red leaf.
A train with white cars departs.
I walk outside and hear nothing.
Inside, footsteps in a corridor.
Someone has bundled leaves
into circular bales. From fresh dirt
small green sprouts, hopeful
before winter.

Between Waking and Rising

Yesterday I carried a quail with a broken beak
into the tall creek grass. Later, rain pounded
my porch roof. The bird floated by smiling

and spinning in the brown current. A baby-faced man
living in my chicken coop stood in the downpour
shaking a scabby fist. *Lord let me have wings.*
I taped a fish to the window to let me feel

underwater also. A cloud of rain came into
my kitchen. My brother found me on the curb
playing cars in the gutter. The bird's
beak catches a twig and the creek swallows it.

The man's fist bleeds into the creek and
the creek into the gutter. My brother opens
the door of a red station wagon and I get in.

Out the back window, blood dots the highway
and birds dive into cement. Who could believe
in this two inches of time that a soul could
choose to live? It's a wonder the trees

don't cast their branches into the earth, that
the houses and chicken coops and roofs don't
disassemble and refuse. Each day I move through

a falling. I met my bald baby when I was a child
driving a car in the gutter of blood.

Love and Ease

A large man on a sunny sidewalk says
Whatever it was I guess we didn't do it.

It's true we're full of what's not.
A large man inside me is shouting
it's undone. A thin man tap dancing shakes
an empty cup. Step up! The Hangman winks.
The Magician lights his rabbit on fire.

The sidewalk blazes like a star
burning out.

•

It rains on and off.
Ghost irises hover.
Giant tulip cups fill.
Baby birds holler
under eaves.

I drink wine all day
and the world slips
into place.

Sunflower Forest

through green trunks
covered with white fuzz
a small creek winds

a birch bird house
hangs from a clothesline

tiny shirts fill
with breeze

the current breaks
on glassy rocks

half a seed
with a cloth sail
bumps down creek

a root boom swings

there is no sailor
and no mate though fifty

suns bend their
tired necks and peer into

the empty little world

The Fairy

A fairy reclines
on a white
bench smoking

sunflowers shadow
his pocked face
and drooping shoulders

a bee hovers
inside a spotted
foxglove flower

the fairy
stubs the butt
against the bench

just as the bee
zooms out
of the blossom

*I don't belong
here* he mutters
and buries

his face in his
grubby hands

Where I've sprinkled seeds

a milky way of green
crosses the garden

daisies rise
from crannies in the path
their spare limbs like wires
without cloth

a gray cat
chin deep in young sunflowers
listens to buzzing
particles of air

garlic
multiplies under earth
and grass root parts tiny
globes of dirt

along the chicken
wire fence vines of giant moon
flower choke the bright
pea blossoms

night drops grains of mist
like cells in a lilac hive
irises and tulips
shut their cups

and the white faces
of the moon flowers open
to the cold scattering galaxy

Slowness

Some of us fall behind,
drag our coats like heavy shadows.
Our hands curl inward
when we try to write. We struggle
even to tie our shoes.
Shy and incapable, we are
terrible swimmers, tired treaders.
Crawl is impossible,
breaststroke a challenge, butterfly
beyond imagination.
                    It doesn't
matter that our mad
fluttering strengthens our wings,
that our desperate hands
trying harder to speak
grow wise.

We are trodden upon and mocked
even by ourselves.

My shadow takes a step ahead
turns back and laughs
at me carrying a misbuttoned
winter coat inside out.
Snow falls but I
can't get the right hand in the right
sleeve. One sad leaf
clings to a thin branch.

Once I stood for hours, my back
to the water, a blunt
swimming instructor yelling

now! and *now!* and *now!*
I will not dive when
I cannot see the surface.
I may not be able to sharpen
a pencil or write without
smudging my paper,

but I have learned
to retreat and refuse.

The New Sentence

Each morning I jump
again. What if all the clocks
are different and I'm

an hour late or a day early?
Who will be waiting

for me? I remember this place
from an inked map
bled into a white napkin,

the Kansas curves and dusty
fields and white
sheep dogs loping like dreams.

If I were a sheep
I would want dogs like that
to lead me. I would want

someone to corral
my clocklessness as if
it were art.

I would want clouds
bending toward me,
and my name

written on the surface of ponds
and someone to read it.

But here on the edge
of the sheep dog's map
the world is like a new

sentence, and I, lucky sheep,
must begin.

Swimming

Your left wing
caught on a nail

beside the door
Here! It's a tiny door!

The wing's
torn and corded
veins rise like red

and blue rivers.
White caps
bob like birds

their eyes
distant targets.

And there's you!
floating on your back

your sore wings
hanging.

Exile

Winter is the silence
after your death

your ghost
blanketing the trees

the sheathed heron
reaper of stillness

handler of a sickle moon
bends her head

I listen for my breathing
as your spirit

leaps toward me

the only joy I want
is the joy of grief

sorrow's whitest snow

Appalachian Spring

hope is a river
that does not freeze

though ice stacks
like steps on its banks.

hope is winter's white star
the comic

snow strip of a branch's
tragic mask.

peer through my frozen globe:
the Hierophant

has killed the cat.
one floor below the lonely Fool
dances on.

Possum dreams upside down
in a coat made of snow.

September

The September sunflowers
look so sad
I want to push
their petals
from their drooping
faces *you're still beautiful*
I whisper

the weight of their despair
hangs
like low clouds
soon snow
will bury the last
clown poppy

and my face
now full of sadness
will stare at the fading
sky as if
from under ice

you're still beautiful
whispers the magpie

hopping across the snow
leaving quiet and temporary
footprints

Naming

is an empty canning room,
the shelves deep

with the circles
of jars burned into them.

Memory is a night sky,
ghosts stalking a blackboard.

Giant fish leap and fall
into an ancient murk.

The stars are a fog
with no eyes.

There is nothing here
worth remembering.

Some days will remain silent.

Resignation

Dusty people
live in the ocean's snowstorm
where bits of foam
flee like birds.

The tide swallows
a black duck with a broken wing

and we walk on.

Christmas Pageant for Peace, 2001

The future
is the underside of a bell,
winter and broken
clusters of light.

It is skeleton coral
and the vacated
necks of barnacles.

The president stands
on a ladder and lights
an exploding star.

The cow donates her ribs
for the bars
of a xylophone.

The future
marches in and empties
its belly,

steaming piles of coins
in the deep snow.

Ms Chisolm's Red Jacket

Elizabeth Chisolm
died and I

wear her jacket
in the rain

indifferent to distance
and time.

Disease slips in the doors
each death leaves open.

Each sadness has flung wide
the windows.

The immune system
wants to live

like a child in a downpour
waving a fist at the sky

and stamping her red foot.

Ace of Cups

I am paused
on my steps holding
a blue cup

bulbous clouds
gather in the shape
of a carp

Green coins
flip in wind

and water
runs over my hands
I bend my head

and stare
into the fountain

When You're Gone

Your cup
is half full.

Lilypads of white
mold float there and

small cloudy spores
hang over the surface.

I forget to clean
when you're gone. Mostly

I watch puffs
on the air

and tiny bugs
turn to dust in the night.

Lullaby

The moon wanders wheat paths
and sad stars wave and blink.

A baby in a boat
imagines their lives. The boat's nose

cuts dark. The moon
is the underside of a trashcan where

spotlights of streetlamps
streak the sky.

The moon is a wafer, a lily,
a flash. When you turn over the coin

your face always looks back.

THE LAST DAY OF JANUARY

Blue King

The Blue King
stares at his feet
dug into sand, Blue King
can't eat—too sad. What
does the Blue King dream? He
dreams of steam rooms and
hospital robes and pillows
like clouds. He dreams of
dead men smiling and legs
in bathtubs, heads in hallways.
He dreams of fingers in his
pudding and dirty toes
with yellow curling nails
tucked under his pillow.
Pudding, Blue King calls.
Stuff me with pudding
to sleep.

What the Trashcan Said

Two small white angels
stand on a street corner.
An old man with crab claw
hands grasps one
by the wing and
swings it into a trashcan.

The second angel
puts on a fake
nose and beard
and disappears
into the crowd.

Oh Crab Man!
cries the first. Take me
to the sea. Trade these
wings for a trip
downstream. But how
can an angel like me dream
when I cannot wake?

The trashcan replied,
He's nothing but an old man
with crab claw hands.

Fierce at the Sky

Your sister
gets cancer, treats it
with prayer
and dies

emaciated and murmuring.
You hope she will have
angels.

This happens to
everyone. I am one

blue moon festival
from full bloom.

I ferry my sister
to the shore, stab
my pole in the blue murk

and turn away.

The Third Hurricane

As you lay dying
God wept violently

and blew his nose twice.
As you lay wasting,

he flattened a Port Charlotte
trailer park, flooded Flagler Beach,

rendered 26 million people
blind. But he never

knelt beside your bed
or touched your hand—

so you died. God inhales
and we wait.

The Thinker

My sister scratches her
skull with a tiny
bony hand,
the Thinker thinking

her tiny translucent thoughts.

Her enormous
eyes roll back and the whites
shake with seizure.

Tiny brown teeth,
a permanent October grin.

My sister's body
is covered with the finest thickest
hair, her eyes encircled

by death's mascara.
Her tiny head
nods again and again

and again. Her eyes
spin like slot machine tags,
settle and stare,

blind and alien and clear.

The Crone

I wake in a city.
Bodies cover the snowy streets.
The left over

halves of people bend
their heads against their chests.

In complete dark,
I rest my infected eyes.

My dead sister
sits at my bedside moving

my hair from my face,
wiping my forehead with a dead
cloth.

I am a tree. I am a crone.
I stare into the flaring fire.

I stand in a basement
filled with brown water.

I meet my sister at a carnival.
Holding hands, we run into the crowd.

I'm standing in a glass ball
filled with fog.

I turn and turn and turn.

The Greening

Dragonflies wear green slippers
and small pink hats. Faces

hide in trees and a boy with horns
dances down a yellow path.

Light illumines the palest leaves
and branches turn to firesticks

from which fairies swing. When a great
sadness presses me into pavement,

I come here to rest in green
and a little man with horns leans over me.

It is a wonderful dream at first. Then
he is mean and drunk,

and his yellow leaves turn
to bile. Pinched faces of the fairies

appear between lacey wings
whizzing like the far

sounds of planes.

The Knocking

I pull you from fog,
my hands lost

in your borders. Fog
inhabits me
like a knocking I won't answer.

I pull you out of a well,
and my hands
turn black and boundary-less.

The knocking too
has no end, a circle

without center,
art without a lie.

I still refuse to answer.

the bridge the conference woman is building

is unfinished but
the ghosts—
the man with two
mossy teeth, the tabby
who died crossing the street,
the conference woman's
parents and even the conference
woman herself
with her small red bag—
are smashing
the traffic cones and
dismantling
the fences.

Everyday Wickedness

Here comes the butcher
with his burlap sack.

Here comes the widow
carrying a lamp.

The orphan sleeps with his head
in the drunkard's lap.

In a pasture of parts, horses
graze, and soldiers

stagger home in the dark.
Here comes the butcher relentless

as night. All the jugs are empty,
except for the wine.

Turn the lamp over,
look through the rain.

War leaves mementos
like fingers in a sack.

Gather children, widows and men.
Here comes the butcher

whistling again.

Hospital Dance

My sister knows she's dying
and that is why
she's dancing in her hospital gown

tapping a cane on the hard wood floor.
And when she died,
she thought she was still alive.

In my dreams we both know
better.

The Last Day of January

I visit the amphitheatre
at Morbid Pond. The ground is gauzy with snow's
left over netting. Red limber trees circle us.

I sit on one of many logs, the theatre's
scattered benches. All around me small men
in black paper hats catcall and clap. Morbid Pond

has shrunk to a disc of soft ice the size of a manhole.
Somebody's knocking but I won't open the door. The air,
thick and dizzy, smells of sap and leaves.

There is no program, the men wave nothing
but their hands. There is no beginning to this show.
There's only an end.

The River People

The river people float asleep
in their basements. Birth

happens every night.
Their grass homes never burn
but shine.

Killings do not change
the dreaming and floating.

Impervious, they
clap their green hands.

Hey diddle diddle
the rat stole the fiddle
and the party marches on.

Comets turn to stars
and stars to comets
and counting always goes wrong.

The river people wear their green
hats like crowns.

The river is grim
and still the river people
hang their green jackets to dry.

Turn them inside out
and turn them outside in,
the river people

are the shine in a dead man's eye.

Acknowledgments

Confrontation: "Florida Morning"

Hanging Loose: "the old city," "Blue King"

Chattahoochee Review: "The Crone"

Louisville Review: "The Knocking"

Whitefish Review: "Where I've Planted Seeds"

Railtown Almanac: Spokane Poetry Anthology: "The Last Day of January," "The River People"

Dual Coast Magazine: "Beaten Blues"

Green Hills Literary Lantern: "After You're Gone" (Pushcart nominated), "Morning Wash"

Cascadia Review: "The Thinker," "The Last Day of January," "Savior," "The River People"

Cirque: "Exile"

MO: Writings from the River: "Landscape"

Cranky: "The bridge the conference woman is building"

Redactions: "Ferry Ride," "The Fish Devour Us," "Nocturne" (now part of "Between Winter and Spring")

Hubbub: "Ms. Chisolm's Red Jacket"

Poets Against the War website: "Christmas Pageant for Peace"

Heliotrope: "Night Life," "September"

Candlelight Bard: "Easter Morning"

Snow Monkey: "MoonBoy," "Here in the White Room"

Rain: "We Need the Rain"

Point No Point: "The Big Sky"

Exquisite Corpse: "Baby's Gone Away"

Upper Left Edge: "315 West Marine Drive"

Albatross: "Middle Beach" (excerpted in *Poet's Market*)

Kalliope: "Hotel Florida"

Special thanks to everyone who read and gave me feedback on these poems and this manuscript over so many years: Christopher Howell, Steve Cleveland, Heath Herrick, Barbara Hansel, Sandee Meade, James Nolan, Peter Meinke and anyone else I might be missing.